Dude, Seriously,

It's NOT All About You!

"Dare to stand out
from the herd"

by

Susan P. Ascher

Joe –
Yes, it
is all about you Now!
Best –

WP

Woodpecker Press, LLC
Bayville, NJ

Dude, Seriously,
It's NOT All About You:
"Dare to stand out from the herd"

Copyright © 2011 by Susan P. Ascher. All rights reserved.

Published by
Woodpecker Press, LLC
P.O. Box 316, Bayville, New Jersey
www.WoodpeckerPress.com
info@woodpeckerpress.com

ISBN: 978-0-9841516-7-7 (sc)
ISBN: 978-0-9841516-6-0 (ebk)
ISBN: 978-0-9841516-8-4 (ebk)

Printed in the United States of America
Hoboken, New Jersey

Cover design: Hit Designs, www.hitdesigns.com
Author photograph: JanPress/PhotoMedia, www.janpress.com

Dedication

This book is dedicated to the three most important women in my life:

My grandmother, who taught me that character and good manners are what you develop when no one is watching;

My extraordinarily loving and kind mother, who brought new meaning to the word Herzensbildung (def. nobleness of the heart);

and

My wonderful daughter, whose sensitivity and compassion for those around her always makes me proud.

Table of Contents

Introduction

Emily Post would be rolling in her grave if she knew how much the world has changed since she wrote her first book in 1922, entitled *Etiquette in Society, in Business, in Politics, and at Home*. It was a best seller, back in the day, and updated versions continued to be popular for decades. Times have changed.

Who cares where the oyster fork is or if I wear whites on the tennis court? Or if my date walks closest to the street so as to keep the splash of a rain puddle from dirtying my raincoat? Most people don't even know which side their bread plate is supposed to be on, or their water glass, for that matter.

It's funny. I hear people complaining about how we as a society have lost our way when it comes to manners. And yet, the other day, I was having coffee with a friend at the local Dunkin' Donuts. It was obvious that three little boys (maybe they were eight years old) and their dads had just come from soccer practice. The boys were at one end of the table, shrieking at one another amid mouthfuls of bagels and cream cheese. (Whatever happened to children should be seen and not heard? And chewing with your mouths wide open—NOT?) Their fathers were at the other end, baseball caps on all their heads, and of course, to make sure that they looked cool, with the caps turned backward.

Next to them, coincidentally, was a table of two mothers and their four daughters. All of them were yelling into their cell

1

phones at people who were not at the table. The profanity that the one mother shouted when she spilled her coffee went hand in hand with the back talk of the other mother's teenage daughter, when the mom asked her to bring some napkins to the table.

And all the while, I just kept thinking that, with examples like these for parents, it's no wonder we are out of control when it comes to manners. The problem as I see it is that a lot of folks just think their kids, through osmosis, will learn their manners at school, from television, or better yet, they will find them on their own when they grow up. I don't think so! It is our responsibility as parents, and as a part of society, to teach our kids a modicum of decorum and protocol. If we don't, then who will?

The lack of respect for others is becoming so great that I actually wrote this book as a tool to raise the bar for both my corporate clients and the individuals who represent them in the workplace. With customer care becoming the number one differentiator for companies, knowing how to charm and disarm anyone that you come into contact with, anytime, anywhere, is priceless and reaps rewards well beyond the bottom line.

I was recently at a conference when the guy sitting next to me took the roll off of my bread plate. When I called the waitress over to ask for a fresh plate, he practically screamed at me and said, "How'm I supposed to know?"

Well, guess what? If you don't know, maybe you could ask, or figure out who does know, and follow their lead. Or better yet, sincerely apologize for behaving like a nitwit. Not because you don't know where your plate is, but because you actually don't care to learn something, so that in the future you can consider someone other than yourself. Whew! I'm mad as hell and I can't take you people any longer.

And what about The Elevator Rule? Aka The Subway Rule. Seriously, let's use a little common sense. Why on God's good earth would you get on the elevator before letting me off. I actually do not want to go back up to the twenty-fourth floor, after I've ridden all the way down. More importantly, I have to get off the train, to make room for you to get on the train. I may not want to take the D Line back to where it originated.

I have been thinking about how to tackle a subject that very few people care about anymore. So I decided I would have to think about manners in the context of today—in the context of the new millennium—and try to define what modern manners actually are and how they can actually help us stand out from the herd, help us differentiate ourselves when it comes to getting a job, making friends, and leading less stressful lives.

My daughter tells me nobody cares. But you see, I did, and that's why she has the sensibilities that so many of the people around her lack. I cared about how she was raised and how she treated those around her. She has what my German mother taught us kids: Herzensbildung. You can't really translate it, but when I looked it up online, the definition is "nobleness of the heart."

To be more contemporary, I will quote Spike Lee, the famous director: "Just do the right thing." If we all followed that mantra, aka The Golden Rule, well, then I wouldn't have to write this book! And the world would be a more civilized place.

And what's so great about acting civilized? Well, acting civilized denotes that a culture or, for that matter, a person, is advanced. It's acting polite, well bred, refined. We have certain societal norms. Let's start with an obvious example. People don't run around in the nude (unless they do it at nudist camps, where they pay to do their own thing in the privacy of a place with people of common interests). So it would be considered uncivilized to go out on the street naked.

A not-so-obvious example, and one that tells a lot about how societal norms change, would be when I was growing up. My grandfather, who was a very formal, British-schooled gentleman, disapproved of slang. So one day when I went for a visit, he opened the door and I greeted him with a big, "Hi."

"Hi?" he asked. "What is 'Hi?'—HELLO is the proper word, Suzi," he said. "You sound very uncivilized," he told me.

Well, I'm sure I really wasn't being uncivilized, I was just changing with the times. Although I am certain that I did offend him. And therein lies the difference. Certain norms will never change (nudity) and certain norms change as we evolve as a society (how we communicate, right down to the difference between using snail mail and e-mail).

But politeness and The Golden Rule never go out of style. So now, what about viewing civilized behavior as "polite" behavior? What happened to stopping at a stop sign when you are in your car? Yellow does not mean go faster, it means caution, slow down. But lots of people on our roads think it's just fine to run red lights, tailgate, and cut people off.

Oh, and let's not forget the importance of honking the horn whenever we don't immediately get our own way on the road. Add to that the road rager who will roll down their window (or not) and curse or gesture with one of the fingers on their hand wherever and whenever they don't get the right of way.

Now I ask you, is stressing out like a banshee so you can arrive at your destination two minutes earlier, or maybe two hours later if you happen to cause an accident with your uncivilized, bad behavior, worth it?

Take the flip side. The light you are approaching an eighth of a mile down the road is red. You see that someone is trying to pull out of a parking lot, and you are the only one who can let the guy in. Think about how nice it would be of you to let him in. Think about how less stressed you will feel, letting him in. And think about how civilized and polite you are. It's all good.

We are going to explore basic ways that will not only make you feel better about yourself and those you come in contact with

4

every day, but also disarm and charm those very same people—
every day. You will learn that in this crazy, sometimes nasty and
extremely fast-paced, competitive, it's-all-about-me world we live
in, treating people well is the best revenge!

Susan P. Ascher
June, 2011

Chapter One

Three of Life's Most Important Phrases: Please, Thank You, and I'm Sorry

For those of you who learned the importance of these phrases early on, consider yourselves way ahead of the curve compared to those who didn't. And more importantly, consider yourself lucky! You see, saying please in order to receive something (be it a salt shaker or a huge favor) and saying thank you (when you do receive what it is you asked for) shows a humility that makes the giver feel like they just made you feel good, or helped you out, or returned a favor. But whatever the outcome, humility is charming. And respectful.

On the other hand, not saying those words makes you come across as arrogant, selfish, and disrespectful. So why would anyone want to please you, or make you feel good, or on an even broader scale, hire you or do business with you? It never ceases to amaze me what those three little words (or lack of them) can reap or (spoil). If I'm starting to sound like a broken record, it's not on purpose. It's just that back in the day it was required in my family to use these words as a sign of gratitude or politeness or humility. And if I had even a chance of scoring whatever it is I wanted—a ride to a friend's house, another cookie, a special favor—the only hope I had was if I would say please or thank you.

I remember being so programmed to say please and thank you that when I was hanging out with my best friend and her mother would offer us an after-school snack, I would always automatically say "yes please" and "no thank you" and "yes please" and "no thank you" and well, you get it. My friend would get annoyed because her mother would tell her she should be more like me, and it was just plain irritating to her. What I didn't realize was how, even back then, I was already differentiating myself. I am not telling you this to give off a "mama raised me right" vibe of some brownnosing annoying kid. I was far from that. I am telling you this because the only way a kid learns good manners is through someone doggin' him or her. Those "someones" used to be parents.

After awhile, those "pleases" and "thank-yous" become second nature, and I realize how much people who use them reap, wherever they go.

We all want to be appreciated for what we do, from the barista who is making your latte, to the shampoo assistant who washes your hair, to the kid bagging your groceries. Why don't you make a list of all the people you could say those words to over the course of the day, and I guarantee that not only will you make them feel good about themselves, you will make yourself feel good about you! You'd be surprised how grateful folks in the service industry are when they feel valued. Sometimes they reciprocate by giving special treatment in return.

The last time I had my hair shampooed, I thanked the assistant when she came over to get me for my shampoo. When she finished shampooing, she asked me if I wanted a special conditioner on my hair. I'd have to sit for ten minutes, but it would make it smooth and silky. "How much?" I asked.

"Twenty dollars," she responded, "but you're the only person here who said thanks today, and I want to do something special for you." Wow! Not only did I get preferential treatment, but she got a big tip! And we both felt good. And remember, feeling good and being nice is always the best revenge.

I can give you countless examples of please and thank you.

What about the guy who makes my sandwich at the lunch counter? "You want extra pickles like usual?"

"Yes please," I say. Followed by, "Thank you!"

"Any time!" he says. You all know the expression, it's the little things that count. And saying please and thank you make you a rock star in the game of life, and a superstar in the eyes of the people you touch.

Just the other day, I was on a very long line in at our local specialty coffee store. The woman in front of me stepped up to the server and demanded, "I need a grande, two pumps of vanilla, no sugar, just a little cream, and I'm in a hurry!" Wow, if I ever saw a display of disrespect and bad manners, this was classic. The server's eyes glazed over, and he proceeded to fix the woman's coffee while everyone on line just stared at her in disbelief. The icing on the cake of course was the lack of a tip.

Right after the woman left, the server's partner turned to him and whispered, "Don't worry, she'll be back tomorrow with the same attitude."

The next person in line, a young man who had never been in this particular store before, stepped up to the counter and said hello to the server (thereby acknowledging his presence) before placing his order, which he began with, "May I please have a grande decaf with two sugars?" and followed up with, "And if it's not too much trouble, could you also please make another one just like it, only this time with cream please?" Well, this time, the server couldn't do enough for the customer. "By the way," she said to him, "if you come in a little earlier tomorrow, we have special pumpkin muffins coming in, and I'll give you one to try!"

Try a little sweetness in your approach, as this guy did, and you will surely get a whole lot more than you asked for!

Why is that so difficult for people to understand? When the waitress who stands on her feet all day (for minimum wage plus tips) delivers coffee, and you need more cream, when someone goes out of their way to hold the door for you as you are struggling with grocery packages, and even when you are on your cell phone because your last meeting made you late and you are calling the babysitter when a cop stops you, remember the three most important phrases to get you through the day.

To the waitress: I know you are really busy, but when you get a chance may I please have a little more cream?

To the UPS guy who delivers packages all day long: Thank you so much for holding the door for me, I really appreciate that.

And to the cop who just pulled you over (and before you want to blow a gasket), try this one (it has always worked for me) as you roll down the window in a panic: "I am so sorry officer." You may not get a reduced ticket, and you obviously broke the law by talking on the cell while driving, but you never know. I am no angel when I am behind the wheel, but I have always managed to get a lesser ticket, simply because I uttered those three little words: I am sorry.

Which reminds me of a story of a friend of mine who regularly got stopped by a cop because he was always speeding. A very high-strung individual, he would see the glare of the lights and hear the sounds of the siren, and expletive deletives were already coming out of his mouth when the officer approached the car. "What did I do?" he would scream. Well, you know the rest of the story: license, registration, $200 ticket.

Me, on the other hand, my first name is Multitasker. And my last name is Rush. So it's no wonder that I occasionally (like once a year or so) will get stopped by a police officer. And as he approaches me in the vehicle, what do I do? I take two deeps breaths, and I say, "I'm so sorry, officer." Truth be told, the only thing I ever got from a police officer after he stopped me was a written warning—from cell phone error, to speeding ten miles above the limit, to doing a California roll. I am not advocating violating any of these regulations, I am only stating the fact that no matter who you are dealing with, from a waitress, to the guy on the street, to a police officer, saying please, thank you, and I'm sorry are still the best phrases to get what you want.

Here are a bunch of everyday examples of when to say please and/or thank you:

1. When you order your java, your sandwich, your gas at the pump, or whatever it is you're ordering.
2. When someone holds the door for you.
3. When you ask your assistant for something.
4. When the waiter pours the water, goes over the specials, delivers your meal, clears the table, or presents your check.
5. When the FedEx/UPS guy/gal delivers a package.
6. When the FedEx/UPS guy/gal picks up a package.
7. When someone gives you a gift (this will be discussed in a separate chapter).

Now it's your turn. On the next page, please list seven examples of when you can say please or thank you. This will help to get you in the habit of doing so on a regular basis. Try it. You'll like it. And the people who are the recipients of your charm will love it.

The people I should say please and thank you to are:

1. _____

   _____

2. _____

   _____

3. _____

   _____

4. _____

   _____

5. _____

   _____

6. _____

   _____

7. _____

   _____

Chapter Two

Netiquette: Our Manners on the Internet

Oh boy, how much time do I have?

Very succinctly, let's start with a simple premise: how you write an e-mail defines who you are. An e-mail is a human exchange. Just because you cannot see the person does not give you carte blanche to be unprofessional or impersonal, or a raging lunatic. Let me tell you about the e-mail I received from a client.

But I need to set up the story so you can understand my shock and disbelief. We are in the temporary staffing business. Years ago, this particular client worked for us. Yes, she was a contract temporary at one of our clients. That means my signature was on her paycheck, and I was her employer, boss, big kahuna. More importantly, she was grateful to have the work during the recession that occurred right after 9/11/2001.

Fast forward to 2010. After I reconnect with her on LinkedIn, she finally calls me to engage our firm. After I start the search for these impossible-to-find candidates, she sends me the contract (that's a good thing) and tells me to check out the requirements on the Web site (not good, as there is usually a lot of background information along with the stuff on the Web site). I do so and leave her not one, but two voice mails to discuss.

A week goes by and she never sends me any particulars, as was promised. She then calls me to find out how we are doing. It was just before six PM. I was on another call on my cell, and on my way to a board meeting. I said I would call her back on the number in my cell. She agreed. Well, guess what folks? It was a trunk number for her company, which does not accept incoming calls since it's in a conference room. Anyway, short story long, I thought the number on my cell was her office number, and that's where I subsequently tried to reach her. Then I got smart and called the main number, and they patched me through to her real office number. So now I call and call that number before I decide to go back to the main number, where I get to her voice mail, and say that I have been having trouble reaching her, and could she please get back to me. Oh, and by the way, since two days had gone by, I also e-mailed her with a read receipt notification to make sure that she read it. Remember, I can be a Pollyanna sometimes, and I don't want my clients to ever be angry or disappointed in me.

So here's what I get in return—and after you read it, I will go into all the salient points of why writing stuff in an e-mail better be well thought out, or it can cause all of us loads of unnecessary problems. Here goes:

> Susan: I am prepping for a big meeting that is taking place tomorrow, so I do not have any more time to spend with you today or tomorrow. I have downloaded plenty of information to you by now, so please just submit the candidate first in Taleo and then e-mail to me if you want my immediate review. If you have concerns, then outline them in your email.
>
> Also, please note my correct office number below. The reason you were having trouble reaching me is that when I left you a message on your cell phone, I was calling from one of our conference rooms. That is why you were having trouble getting back to me. But in the future, check your information first before calling me or complaining that I am not reachable.

Now mind you, she did call me back and subsequently e-mail me. The problem is (she must be so very important) that she never sent me an e-mail with her autosignature. Therefore, I only had the main number of her current employer, and that's where I always called.

But, you should have heard the absolute rudeness in her tone. She must not have a lot of power except over those that she thinks she can boss around. Suffice it to say that I took a deep breath. In the twenty-five years I had been in business, I had never had a client address me in the tone that she had addressed me in. I was speechless. I decided I would sleep on it before answering. And when I got some clarity the following day, I put on my big girl pants, sent the resume, and the rest was history. We placed the individual, and then I fired her as a client! That was probably the third one I've ever done that to. Any relationship, even a business relationship, involves respect. Employer to employee. Employee to employer. Coworker to coworker. And of course, supplier to client. Client to supplier.

Enough about her. The point of the story is that once you put something down in writing, it's there for posterity. "Paper is patient," my mom used to say. So in the green world of e-mail, so is the e-mail and the server that keeps it there via disaster recovery firms. So be dang sure that your tone is professional, courteous, and respectful. There may be rare times in your life when you need a good rant in an e-mail; just make sure the rant is taken in the spirit you mean it, and that the person is someone who you will not potentially offend.

Now as for greetings, and how we address someone in business in an e-mail. Unless it is someone that you are constantly in touch with, or know very well, a salutation such as Good morning Mary, Dear Tom, or (if you know your audience intimately) Hi Amy is in order because it shows that you are not just acknowledging the person, but that you are showing respect for that person. Equally important is how you sign off. Again, Thank you in advance, Sincerely, Best, or Warm regards show that you are closing your e-mail with a respectful good-bye. Acknowledging someone in an e-mail is just as important as acknowledging someone's presence in a room, which is why I always tell my staff that I am not complete until they say hello or good-bye when they come in in the morning or leave at the end of the day. (More on that in Chapter Eleven.)

Now, back to our e-mails. When you are working on a project with a peer, the greeting and sign off can be much more simple, and just first names used. But for goodness sake, use names!

Now, to all the stuff that can go wrong in the body copy. Slang is not acceptable at work. No. Not. Never. Just make it a rule, and you will never have to deal with the aftershock of a managing partner or VP getting wind of your indiscretion. *Hey, dude, what's up with the new marketing plan?* is not cool. It's cool if we are making plans to see a movie with a bunch of pals, but not for the eyes of the chief marketing officer.

And another thing. Before you include anyone whose title appears in caps after their name, i.e., CEO, CMO, SVP, or EVP (get the picture?), in your group e-mail, you may want to consider the importance of what you are sending. Remember, he/she probably gets 150 to 200 e-mails a day. Just keep it simple and send what is relevant and important. If they are only looking for final input, or you need their help on a particular issue, or they are micro-managers, then fine—include them. The point is to make sure that the recipient of your e-mail actually needs to be included. If not, the final draft usually suffices.

I had an employee who, for some reason, never did figure out that I am not a helicopter manager. That I didn't want to see every single draft in an attachment before the final product, which is all I wanted to comment on, unless there was a specific problem or issue that needed to be addressed.

Speaking of bosses and meetings (or friends and events), my biggest pet peeve is the Reply to All button. Just recently, Jack, chairman of the Harvest Ball Committee from a notable charity I am on, had to schedule a meeting. He sent an e-mail to all ten people asking if Friday at eight or Monday at eight would be the better choice for our next get-together. In came the replies from everyone on the contact list.

"I can do Monday but not Friday," from Jim.

"I can do Friday and not Monday," from Sally.

"I can do both," from Bob.

Honestly, I didn't care when anyone else could do it. Only Jack needed to know, and then he could decide what time the meeting would be held. Wasting bandwidth and precious time hitting the Reply To All button is inappropriate and just creates more junk for our computers to store. Stop the insanity!

Let me give you another example of poor netiquette. I have a friend, or should I say a few friends, who think it is perfectly normal to send inane jokes, political commentaries (which I may or may not agree with), or chain letters. If I break the chain letters, I will ruin their, and all the dozens of other peoples lives included in the chain, because their wishes will not come true. I have asked them to stop. They haven't. Their lives are intact, and my bandwidth and spam is becoming increasingly clogged.

Now to flaming. Just what exactly is flaming? Flaming is an online argument that becomes nasty or derisive, where insulting a party to the discussion takes precedence over the objective merits of one side or another, as defined by *Urban Dictionary*. I would strongly recommend never insulting a person to begin with, but doing it over the Internet has all sorts of bad repercussions. Like the recipient being able to resend or post it to various social media outlets as well as including a whole host of people who shouldn't be involved. Remember, once it's on the Internet, it stays in cyberspace forever.

As for writing a word or words in all caps, well, use them sparingly. Like a good spice, writing in all caps adds a little flavor to your e-mail.

For example, maybe I gave you a goal of one million in sales for the fourth quarter, so that we could meet our sales goal for the year. Or if the audit partner wanted all the financials done before midnight on the thirty-first of the month. Or if Number One Consumer Package Goods Company just adores their new logo. Then, maybe, you could shout in an e-mail. Something like: CONGRATULATIONS TEAM. WE DID IT!!!!!!!! But certainly never in the context of dissing your colleague, as in I CANNOT BELIEVE YOU DIDN'T CALL ME BACK LAST NIGHT!!!!

Do you see the difference? Good. And if you don't, let me be just a tad clearer. Writing in all caps is like yelling at someone. If you want to yell congratulations in an e-mail, I'm down with it. If you just want to yell in your e-mail, well just don't. Because it's unacceptable to do it anywhere, any time, in business.

And while we are on the subject of e-mail communication, or netiquette—who died and proclaimed the telephone a tool for dinosaurs? Sometimes a good phone chat, whether during a negotiation, lengthy discussion, or just to make human contact, isn't such a bad idea after all.

Now that we've covered the basics, let's move on to the gimmes. For those of you who like a little slang, I have just provided it. A gimme is a given. Like in golf. A gimme is a two-inch putt. You know you are going to make it, so it's OK. Fine. Good. As a shortcut. Well, in netiquette, there are a few gimmes.

The most obvious is Spell Check. It's a gimme. You have to use it. No excuses. You look like a nitwit if you don't. Sorry for the tough language, but I am a big believer in tough love. I want you to be the best you can be at school, in business, in your personal dealings with those with whom you come into contact.

And for Pete's sake, please don't use "r" and "u" instead of the real words. Oh, and by the way, if you do, adhering to the first gimme, Spell Check, will insure that you don't.

As for smiley faces, emoticons, all that good stuff, save them for your girlfriend, your mom, or your kid. No place for it in college or in business.

Well folks, if you are still with me (and I presume you are, because this stuff is kind of fun and important to know), let's never forget that our personal e-mails are just that. If I want to moan about the long meeting my boss just had, I am going to do it from my personal e-mail, to my friend's personal e-mail. I am NEVER [yes, that was for emphasis—just making a point to my students (you)], never going to do that from my business e-mail address. Nor would I ever send questionable materials, be they political, off-color, or nasty.

Don't forget that everything you ever write is on someone's server. Ollie North learned that. If you don't know who he is, look him up on *Wikipedia*. I'm not an expert at history, just an expert in niceness. The bottom line on Ollie is that just because you delete something, if an investigation is ever required, they will find it. Everything we write in an e-mail is on someone's server. If you don't want it on the company bulletin board, don't put it in an e-mail.

So let's just sum it up, for those of you who prefer CliffNotes™.

- Your e-mails define you.
- Check, check, Spell Check.
- Do not flame!
- Do not write in ALL CAPS unless it is to emphasize or congratulate!
- Personal for personal.
- Business for business.
- No slang.
- Everybody's last deleted e-mail is on someone's server.
- If you don't want it on the company bulletin board, don't put it in an e-mail.

Chapter Three

Be Careful Navigating Cyberspace and Social Media

S lapping up pictures of last night's frat party with you, a bud, and a Bud, making lewd gestures while half dressed, may have seemed fun and funny at the time, but, dude, seriously, one of your 500 friends may just have a connection you weren't thinking about. Or, better yet, what exactly were you thinking? One of those 500 friends may just happen to be your next-door neighbor's mother, or your boss, or maybe even one of your professors. Why do you think Mark Zuckerberg is a gazillionaire? We may all know that famous concept that we're all within six degrees of separation, but Zuckerberg figured out that we are merely a nanosecond away from lots of people wandering around in cyberspace.

So to all of you peeps out there who think nobody can see you, let's not forget that if we are not vigilant when it comes to our privacy settings, they easily become piracy settings. Don't tell me you've never creeped anyone. What about your roommate who didn't invite you to his wedding because you had a falling-out? There they are, all of your fraternity homies, slurping martinis from an ice fountain at his bachelor party. What about the nice one of him and his future wife last summer on the beach in Nantucket? Now think about all of the other people out there who might be creeping you. And one may even be Monday morning's interviewer for that highfalutin job at that Wall Street firm you've been trying to get hired by.

I know, I know—you're above it all. That only happens to other folks. And so what? What's the big deal? Well, dude, it really is a big deal. Anything we put on social networks such as Facebook, Myspace, and even the business network, LinkedIn, is out there for the world to see and then to judge you on. And speaking of business social networks, that's what they are. Key word: business. Only post a professional picture, please. And, no, you may not friend your boss on Facebook. No. Not. Never. If it is company policy to be on LinkedIn, make sure you keep your communications with colleagues to a minimum. Let everybody else risk job and paycheck to join group discussions. The written word in cyberspace (or anywhere on the computer for that matter, as we learned in Chapter Two) is very patient. It will just sit there forever and ever, and if something was said that teed off a coworker, or boss—trust me, it'll be there for everyone to see. Not good.

Which brings me to the subject of twits and tweets. OK, OK, I know you're a cyberspace force to be contended with and really need a Twitter account. Until you become a savvy, experienced business person, however, leave the tweets to others, or you may be viewed as a twit. Who cares when you last brushed your teeth, hair, dog? Or how much you drank last night? Unless you just released your first platinum CD, leave the coolness to the rock stars and get over your lame life. Move on, open a book, be first in your class, or land (or keep) the best job on the planet.

Chapter Four

Filters: Aka What Were You Thinking?

For those of you unfamiliar with the term filter, *Urban Dictionary* (the online dictionary of the same name that features a cornucopia of slang words and phrases) defines filter as "An intangible device that determines which thoughts to actually say out loud to another human being." Most, not all, politicians have filters, as they are always trying to be perceived as someone we should like, and then vote for. So (with exceptions) successful politicians try to take negativity out of their oratory. They cater to the audience of the given moment they are in, and are masters of filtering, for the most part.

There are exceptions to the rule. One would be Carl Pelligrini (*Wikipedia* or Google can define who he is better than I can), who ran for governor of the state of New York in 2010 after saying that he didn't believe in gay marriage, even though some of his staff and best friends are gay. Somebody call 911! And get the man a filter. Tied for not knowing how to filter his words would be Kanye West. First, he accuses President George Bush, back in 2005 during Hurricane Katrina, of being a racist because he didn't care about New Orleans and all of the (mostly) black people dealing with the tragedy.

Another classic case of nonfiltering was when he grabbed the microphone from Best Female Video winner, Taylor Swift, back in September of 2009 while she was thanking the audience for her award. He then goes on a rant about how Beyonce's video was just as good if not better. YIKES! Filter time! Now, to make matters worse, he surfaces again right after George Bush goes public with his memoirs, *Decision Points*. By the way, this is not an advertisement for the former president or his book. He may have made some unpopular decisions during his presidency, but being a racist was never one of them. The anger and sadness in President Bush's eyes when he was interviewed by Matt Lauer of NBC about the incident were obvious. He simply stated, "I didn't appreciate being called a racist. I am NOT a racist." He said it was an all-time low for him during his tenure. Lesson to be learned: Filter thyself.

But, no sooner is the interview out, but Mr. West gets his PR folks to corner Matt on NBC with a comeback. But instead, it backfires, he feels "trapped," and then takes his ball and runs away by canceling what was an upcoming concert on the show. The lack of filter continues as the singer goes on a Twitter rampage. Oh, and one more thing. West excuses himself by saying we have to understand that's what happens when people get emotional.

Really? Other things happen, too. Like taking out guns and shooting people because you don't like them laying you off. Get it? Got it? Good. Filter thyself.

And in third place for a filter story, my own personal one. Let me set it up for you. I am on a short holiday visiting friends in Florida when I get invited to a very important Chaines des Rotisseurs wine tasting. Guests are introduced around the room, and when it's my host's turn, they introduce me as Susan Ascher from New Jersey. I hear strange whispers from the next table. "Ascher," they say. Ascher is my former married name. Michael Ascher is my ex. Important factoids to remember. Another is that while I am a baby boomer, I am always told I look (and act) younger than my years. Two seconds later, a woman I have never seen before pops up from her chair, runs over to my table, and blurts out, "Are you Michael Ascher's mother?"

Mother? God help me! I put on my best finishing school charm, smile, and say, "No, actually Michael is my ex." And as I was processing the fact that only I could be 950 miles away from home and meet Wife Number Two's best friend, while I can't even meet Mr. Right or his distant cousin, Mr. Right Now, in the local Dunkin' Donuts, my filter came on. As she told me her best friend (back in New Jersey) was now married to Michael, she went on to say that she speaks so highly of me. And my daughter is beautiful. And what am I doing in Florida? I must say, I couldn't have acted more like debutante at a cotillion ball (*Wikipedia*). I smiled graciously, said that it was a pleasure to have met her, and when I went to the ladies room three minutes later, saw that my daughter had already texted me. She said she had heard that Wife Number Two had received a phone call from BFF (best friend forever). And the reason I wasn't surprised? Because BFF needs a filter.

Bottom line: In our 24/7 nanosecond society, take a second (or two) to think about what you are going to say before you say it.

Chapter Five

Elevators and Doors

So it's like this. I get on the elevator on the twenty-fifth floor, or maybe the fourth, or even the fifteenth—it doesn't matter. What matters is that when the door opens, I get off, and then you get on. For some obscure, unbeknownst, and incomprehensible reason, people just don't get it. No, seriously, I just came from the top of the building, or maybe I'm going up. Who cares? What I care about is making room for you so that you can get on. Maybe you don't get it. Let's try another example. I am leaving the building. I open the door, and boom! You walk right into me. No, dude. I am leaving. Only when I leave, can I make room for you to come in. Better yet, anybody out there remember the days of holding the door for others? I know. I know. That was back in the medieval days, when chivalry was still alive. And speaking of chivalry, you don't have to be a guy to be nice and open the door for someone who's leaving the office. Or Starbucks. Or the post office. Just treat people like you want to be treated.

It's not that hard! You should try it. Most of the time, you'll feel good about it. Sometimes you won't. But let's not forget good ole Spike Lee's mantra, do the right thing. Aka The Golden Rule. For those of us born after the dinosaur age, and some of us born during it, treating people well is the  best revenge. It's startling. It's disarming. But most of all, it's charming. And in case you never figured this out on your own, charming people very often get their own way, in spite of the nasties they encounter in life. Not so terrible, eh?

This reminds me of a Tuesday morning a few years ago when I was playing team paddle tennis. I had an early match and didn't have time to make coffee. My internal navigation told me that if I kept right on going, I would make my court time exactly fifteen minutes before my match. But alas, the caffeine junkie in me just had to stop at the Dunkin' Donuts that miraculously appeared at the traffic light on the right side of the road. I slammed on the breaks and tore out of the car only to see two little old ladies teetering on their canes twenty yards ahead of me. And yes (you got it!), I couldn't help myself. I waited and waited, what seemed like an eternity, while they hobbled up to the door. Imagine the look of gratitude on their faces when I held the door for them. They thanked me profusely, and insisted I go ahead of them. OK, so call me Pollyanna. I've been called far worse. But I can tell you this: I did a nice thing. I did the right thing. And I felt great about it. Sure I was pressed for time, aren't we all? But at least I made someone else's day. Now, that's what I'm talking about!

Chapter Six

Cell Phones and Cell Yell

There is a guy in my office building. Let's call him Rob to protect his identity. I think he is the most important person on the planet. As far as I can tell, I think he is more important than the President of the United States, the Queen of England, or the Sultan of Brunei. I say this because whenever I see him, he is walking around with his Bluetooth stuck in his ear. Mostly he is talking about Sunday night's football score, and how awful the fumble looked, and how the Giants, the Redskins, or the Patriots could have won if only—blah, blah, blah. If only he had been playing! But occasionally, I do hear him talking about some client, always referred to as a d#ck, ass, or jerk. The client invariably just doesn't get it, or is a complete moron when it comes to the numbers, or is a wuss who can't make a decision. If he is not walking around the halls having these conversations, he is either on the elevator sharing his proprietary information or on his way into the men's room. Since I'm a girl, I can't be sure that he is still carrying on in there, but since he's still talking when he comes out of the men's room, I think it is safe to assume that his virtual office is just that: virtually everywhere!

So okay, what is the point of the story? Nobody, but nobody is that important that he can't have his or her conversations in the privacy of their office. If you really need a break from the space called your office, then for God's sakes, go outside away from other people, and have your conversation there. People on the elevator are not interested in where your hockey game seats are, what time you are having your manicure, or hearing you screaming expletive

31

deletives about your boss. Stop the self-absorption. In a world where everyone is so caught up in looks and attractiveness, let me be the first to tell you (in case nobody else has) that it just looks bad, and sounds even worse. Get over yourself. You're just not that important!

If you actually were the President of the United States, or the Queen of England, or the Sultan of Brunei, you wouldn't be having your conversations within earshot of the world, now would you? I don't think so.

Just as important as not roaming around the planet with the phone in your ear at all times is considering the ears of the person you are speaking to. I would like to say "speaking with," but "speaking to" or "speaking at" seems more appropriate, because most people on their cell phones are guilty of something known as cell yell. If you are not familiar with the term, then you may be familiar with the term broadcast mode. These terms refer to screaming into the personal digital assistant, usually with the refrain, "Can you hear me now?" to make sure the guy on the other end of the phone is still there. Never pausing except to hear them say yes.

Peeps in broadcast mode resemble evening news anchors in that they drone on and on without any breaks except for the commercials. When communicating with these types, I just sometimes have to fight fire with fire by yelling, not once, but at least two or three times, "Stop, stop, stop!" Dumbstruck, they come to a deafening silence so that you get maybe thirty seconds before they interrupt and the cycle starts all over again.

So now, you ask, what to do? Well, we can't change these patterns of behavior in others, but we can try to change them in ourselves. First off, who ever said we have to be available 24/7 via iPhone or Blackberry? If you don't pick up the phone, maybe they will get the message that (a) you are not available or (b) you are in a public place where you don't want to be heard. When you call them back, you can state reason a or b, and maybe they will get it.

Listening and exchanging are great, productive forms of communication. Broadcasting? Leave that to the network anchors.

Chapter Seven

Landline Telephones

Wow—they really do still exist, and some people still talk on them! The rules are the same though, cell or landline.

No matter who you are making the call to, be it the client, the store, the bank, the restaurant, or wherever, ingratiate yourself. Say, *This is Susan Ascher calling, may I please speak to John Doe?* Or if you are not familiar with a name, ask for "the person in charge of reservations" or "the bank manager," depending on the nature of your call. Amazing that just stating your name makes some people think you actually are someone important. Identifying yourself is not only nice, but it's disarming, and we all know that disarming is charming. Please and thank you sprinkled in for good measure, and there you have it!

Now, as far as making that cold call in business, why not ingratiate yourself with the gatekeeper? If you have been trying to get through to Mr. or Ms. Important, always remember to make their gatekeeper feel as important as you want that prospective client to feel. Start off by asking their name, and make them your partner in getting through to the powers that be. But again, always offer your name, because it shows that you are being genuine and have nothing to hide. Better yet, dude, if you state the reason for your call, you put out there that you are for real and not there to waste anyone's time.

Finally, do me a favor, and stay away from putting people on speaker, unless you have multiple parties who need to be a part of the call. And if you absolutely have to, please make sure that you OK it with the person you are speaking to first, and let them know that your door is closed. Yeah, dude, close the door. No one wants to hear your conversation. Oh, and by the way, never, no, not never, have a speakerphone conversation from your cubicle. That's just plain unacceptable.

One final note on landline etiquette—or any phone etiquette. No chewing food or gum or smoking, of any kind. It's rude, disgusting, and base. (And yes, I can hear you doing it!)

Chapter Eight

Have You No Shame?
Why a Mirror is a Good Investment for
Anyone Not Living under a Rock

C an somebody help me please? When did we go from business attire to business casual to business sloppy? No, seriously. Here's my take on it: back in the day (way back in the day, for you Xer's, Yer's, and New Millenials), guys wore business suits, along with ties, polished shoes, and, like in that now-famous TV show *Mad Men*, fedoras to work. Women wore dresses or suits, depending on their mood or position in the company. Pants in the office were outlawed for us gals, and pantsuits hadn't yet been born. And if you did wear pants, they were called slacks. Which I find very humorous, because slack is the root word for slacker.

I would like the days back when working was actually (no, seriously) nine to five, where girls wore dresses and men wore suits. When men left the office and went home to a three-ounce martini or a home-cooked meal, and women got dressed for dinner. Casual days? They were strictly for Saturdays. Young, sophistocated women of the 1960s would pull out their slacks for shopping or kiddie parties, and in the summer they'd snazz it up with pedal pushers, aka capris, or Bermuda shorts (the ones that skim your knee, not hot pants, as have become the vogue today, regardless of whether you are at the stage where your legs look like cottage cheese—or not). I remember when my mom bought her first pair of pedal pushers. They were bright yellow, and the matching top was an off-the-shoulder boatneck in yellow and black. She looked so sexy and smart that I couldn't even recognize her as my mom. That was 1963. And she only wore that when the family was invited to a neighbor's BBQ on a Saturday afternoon. Other acceptable attire at these events would be sundresses, but never (no, not ever) dungarees. Dungarees, known today as jeans and by some archaic folks as denim, were banned, banished, and a no-no, unless you were working around the house doing activities such as raking leaves or washing windows or cleaning bathrooms. Most of us had mothers whose full-time job was "domestic engineer." Still, they would not venture out in public looking any less than "dressed." Other moms and dads, especially the rich ones, like my best friend's parents, played golf and tennis, and some even rode horses. Funny, you never saw them on the street in their sporting gear, as we do today. All of the attire back then was worn only where appropriate. Tennis togs for the tennis court, suits for the office, dungarees for chores, coat and tie for "after five," and tuxedos and gowns for black-tie functions.

One of the key themes throughout this repertoire of facts and foibles is that manners, etiquette, etc., are really an evolution of society's mores—and even more importantly, tolerances. So while our golf club has loosened weekday dinner attire to "country club casual," it (much to the chagrin of the newest generation) still requires jackets (but no tie) on Saturday evening. The annual holiday ball has demoted its attire requirements to black tie optional in order to include more members in the party. So OK, no problem, times change, and manners and customs do, too. But, there is just no excuse for dressing like you don't care.

But bejesus, if I see one more person with bedhead, in a pair of sweatpants that look like she/he slept in them for the last month, walk into Dunkin' Donuts on any given morning, I am going to lose it. Or a tramp stamp and thong for the whole world to see. Have you no shame, people? OK, I'll say it: its gross, base, declassé, and as my daughter likes to say when someone disgusts her, ewwww. You are in a public place. That means other people have to look at you. Sometimes they even have to smell you. So do me a favor before you leave the house, brush your teeth and comb your hair. Go ahead, make my day—put on a pair of jeans. If you've just finished playing tennis or working out, go home and shower. And if you've no time to do that, then go home and make your own coffee. Starbucks and Dunkin' Donuts both sell it by the bag. Just don't make me have to stand next to you.

Remember, you have thirty seconds to make a first impression—leaving it up to you to decide if that's important.

Chapter Nine

E-mail versus Snail Mail versus Telephone Thank-Yous

Ugh. I've accepted the gift. Or attended the event. Or the party. Or the weekend invite. Most of the time I'm happy to accept the gift or the invite, but now I should say thank you, and I just:

1. Am too busy.
2. Forget.
3. Don't care enough.
4. Think no one will notice (they're busy too).

Answer: None of the above. Wake up and smell the coffee, dudes. There are lots of ways to say thanks, and let me be the first to tell you, if you haven't learned to do it yet, start now! If you're not too busy to accept the gift or the invite, then you can't be too busy to say thanks.

A thank-you can take on many forms. I used to think that e-mail thank-yous were taboo. How dare any of my staff write a thank-you e-mail to a new client after a visit? How dare my daughter e-mail a thank-you to the admissions head when she was applying for college? Well, things change, and e-mail correspondence has become the norm. Notice that I say the norm. Get it? That means normal, run-of-the-mill, mainstream. Sure, there's a time and a place for it in this crazy 24/7 world we live in. So go ahead, follow the crowd and write a thank-you e-mail. But unless it's your bestie, don't even think about texting a thank-you to a client, or your friend's Auntie Betty, or the chair of the last black-tie event you attended.

More importantly, if you want to stand out from the crowd, then please, please, a thousand times please do so. If you just spent the weekend at your friend Kate's summer place in Nantucket, or her Auntie Betty treated you to lunch at the yacht club, surely a handwritten note would be appropriate, wouldn't it? I mean the invite and the setting were standouts, even if Auntie Betty did bore you with the fact that her late husband was an admiral in the U.S. Navy and never felt more at home than when they took their boat down to Palm Beach for the winter, with butler, maids, etc., in tow. So go buy a blank card (maybe go out of your way to find one with a picture of a lovely boat or seafaring setting on the front). Or better yet, get your own customized stationery (you know the kind with the curlicue monograms or just your first name in block letters on the front). And in your neatest handwriting, write a short, sweet thank-you. On the other hand, if you feel creative, print your own personalized cards online. Here, I will help you:

Dear Mrs. (no, not Betty) Bainsbridge,

Thank you so very much for a wonderful time at the yacht club. It was so nice to meet and spend the afternoon with you and Kate. The company was great and the food superb!

I hope you enjoy the rest of your summer, and look forward to seeing you again in the future. Thank you again.

Best regards,

Tiffy

Always make sure your return address is printed on the envelope, or write it neatly on there yourself. Get one of those old-fashioned things called a stamp. You can even buy one online. Better get a few, since you're down with the thank-you note program. Paste it on, and presto! You've done your duty, and maybe Auntie Betty will invite you to stay in her three-story Park Avenue apartment next time you land in Manhattan. (Not that you would necessarily want to, but it would sure beat HoJo's on the West Side.)

Finally, the telephonic thank-you. This is usually employed by the generation known affectionately as "old people." While I hate to admit it, old people are, generally speaking, baby boomers (peeps born between 1946 and 1964), although Gen Xers (those born in the 1960s and 1970s, ending in the late 1970s to early 1980s) can harbor some of the traits of the baby boomers. Anyway, telephone thank-yous once required the user to pick up the phone (these phones were usually found in someone's home or office and are referred to as landlines). People dialed out on them, and when the recipient picked up, they could utter a cheerful hello and comment on what a wonderful day, afternoon, evening, party, lunch, or whatever you threw/had for them and how glad they are that they were invited. Nowadays, most people use cell phones, but the outcome is the same. The telephone thank-you is an easier way of saying thanks, but still acknowledges the fact that the giver of whatever party, gift, etc., is being recognized and appreciated. What a concept! Making people feel important and appreciated by saying thank you.

It's not that difficult when you think about it. The other thing to remember is timeliness. Even though we're all busy with texting, e-mailing, shopping, working, or studying, it's important to keep in mind that if we weren't too busy to accept the invite or the gift, then we have to make a point of getting on board in a reasonable amount of time to say thanks. How could you figure out what a reasonable time frame is? Well, you could put yourself in the role of the giver, and work backward from there. If you had given the gift or threw the party, and put some thought into including someone, what would make you feel good? And that, folks, is the meaning of The Golden Rule. Thanks for letting me explain.

Chapter Ten

Why Gum Chewing, Nose Picking, and Yawning in Public are the Same

Good. Now that I have your attention, the title states three habits that are never (no, not ever) in style.

Now, if you don't agree with my deduction as stated in the title, I would ask you to do a quick experiment. It is preferable if you can video yourself, but standing in front of the bathroom mirror will suffice to get my point across to you nonbelievers. For obvious reasons, ninety-nine percent of humans in our society have been taught early on not to pick their nose. As we say in golf, that's a gimmee. If you disagree, please aim the camera at yourself and shoot yourself pretending you are picking your nose. Dude, tell me you'd never be caught doing that in public! But before I totally close the book on that subject, let's make sure that we know one other thing that is unacceptable relative to nasal habits. And that is, we never (no, not ever) blow our nose into our napkin. As Meryl Streep said in *The Devil Wears Prada*: "That's all. Period."

Now, stand in front of the mirror (or take out the camera again) and stuff your mouth with a wad of gum and start chewing. Now, seriously, make my day. Crack it if you know how, and maybe blow a bubble or two. You think that's cool? Well, you are wrongo wrongo.

If anyone reading this disagrees with me about chewing gum in public (and I know there are tons of you, because you wait on me when I buy a lipstick at Bloomingdale's, or you sit next to me in church or temple, or you even are addressing the audience I'm in during a conference), I would like you to have a friend videotape you while you are doing so. Then have them videotape you chewing your breakfast, lunch, or dinner with your mouth wide open for all to see. Same difference.

The Queen Mother was appalled when Kate Middleton's mother was caught chewing her cud at the Prince's graduation from Sandhurst Military Academy. Now, while I do not think their breakup in 2007 was a result of her mother's bad behavior, it certainly was a wake-up call to any potential girlfriend or fiancée of the Prince. But the real question is why did she have to do that? You are held to a higher order when you become part of the royal family, and as a potential future mother-in-law, you will be scrutinized as much as your daughter. Just like we build character doing the right stuff when no one is watching, we form good habits when we put them into practice everyday. Even if we are not royalty.

In real simple terms, ladies (and gentlemen), please don't chew gum in public. It's really no different from smoking a cigarette in public. Talk about manners reversing themselves, smoking used to be in vogue in the 1950s and 1960s—so much so that it was considered sophisticated to drag on tobacco-filled cancer sticks until, alas, the correlation between the two made people realize it was downright dangerous and bad for your health. In other words, you might die if you get lung cancer from smoking!

Now you probably won't die from chewing gum, but it's also not great for your teeth and gums, but I really don't care about that. Go ahead, chew as much gum as you want in the privacy of your car, your office, or your home. I wish I could slap the girls (funny thing is I have yet to hear a guy crack gum—must be a girl thing) I run into who crack their gum. That is absolutely, positively the worst. My regular manicurist was recently out the day I normally have my manicure done, so Miss Snappy-Cracky was assigned to me. Half the time she's chewing with her mouth open, and the other half she's cracking her gum. If I had a nickel for every crack of gum I've ever heard, I would be sitting on a warm beach somewhere because I would be so rich I wouldn't have to work any longer.

Here's a better one for you. My mother, God rest her soul, was the consummate lady. Mom abhorred the thought of her children doing anything unmannerly. One of the things she despised the most was gum chewing (must be a European thing). We always tried to weasel a piece from our friends, and one time she caught us doing the dirty deed when we were stopped at a stoplight. The man in the car next to us was looking in at us (probably more at my beautiful young mom than at us), and in order to get us to stop chewing she said, with clenched jaw, "Stop chewing or he will think you are talking about him." Like we cared. We were kids, and we were in our own world (much like any gum chewer and/or nose picker usually is). You might not think it's a funny story, but the three of us were howling with laughter (although we had a nice punishment waiting for us when we got home that night, which was no television before bedtime). From then on, there was definitely no more gum chewing in public. Oh how the world has changed!

Here's a little poem that my third grade teacher would recite when she would catch anyone with gum in their mouth in her classroom:

> A gum-chewing boy/girl
> And a cud-chewing cow
> Totally alike, and yet different somehow
> What is the difference?
> Yes! I see it now!
> The intelligent look on the face of the cow!

So seriously, cut it out. You look like a dope, and you sound even worse. Have a little respect, if not for yourself, then for the people who have to watch and hear you while you're doing it. My grandfather's favorite expression (when he caught us not minding our manners), and a mantra I still live by, was, "Act civilized." He was annoying at the time, but now I consider his behavior and knowledge of being a lady or a gentleman the standard to which I want to be held. He simply treated those around him like ladies and gentlemen, and with the same respect he knew all people deserved.

Now the final no-no—yawning, mouth wide open. Here's a test.

Yawning is acceptable in public when you do it in a way so that people:

A) See your tonsils (yuck).
B) View the teeth that you are missing (ewww).
C) Hear you grunt while you do it.
D) See you covering your mouth and excusing yourself; and while so doing, all the while trying to hide the fact that you are doing it.

If you answered "D" you are rare. If you answered anything else, make yourself rare. Let's recap so I know you're still with me. Picking your nose. Gross. Blowing your nose in your napkin. Even grosser. Chewing your food with your mouth open. Yuck. Chewing gum anywhere, anytime (other than in the privacy of your home, car, or office). Unacceptable. Yawning in my face (or anyone else's). Declasse. Knowing that good behavior never goes out of style. Priceless.

Chapter Eleven

Greets, Meets, and Introductions: Aka Acknowledging Someone's Presence

So you are at a business networking event or your friends' holiday open house cocktail party. Someone walks up to you and whoever you are speaking to. Instead of introducing (or reintroducing) themselves, they just start talking to the person you're with, and never even acknowledge your presence. It's not that hard, people. And very important in business and in making the right social connections, as you will learn in this chapter.

I was recently at a charitable event where one of my BFs was the chair and I was a patron. Someone that I have met many times at our golf club walked up to Mary Beth and just started broadcasting whatever she was broadcasting about. I may as well have been a painting or a fixture in the room. Not only did she talk directly to my friend (with an invisible wall between the two of us), she never even acknowledged my presence. My friend, who was being torn in many different directions that evening, with lots of people waving and greeting her during their conversations, assumed that we knew one another. Mary Beth didn't realize that (yet another) introduction was in order for this dimwit.

So I took it upon myself to interrupt politely and say, "Oh by the way, Alexandra, I think we may have met before. I'm Susan Ascher. I think your son goes to my alma mater and I often see you up at the golf club." Looking me up and down, she said hello and continued on as if I didn't matter in the least.

Please promise me that when you are in the company of someone and a stranger or even someone you do know appears, that you will at least say hello and let them know you are aware of their presence. Anyone who shops in Nordstrom knows that when a customer enters a department, even if the salesperson is serving someone else, they must glance over and acknowledge that they are aware of that person and tell them they will be right with them. It makes them feel welcome and like they are visible. I personally do it wherever I go. I smile and say "hey," "hi," or "hello" whether it's the porter in the airport, or my assistant when I greet her in the morning, or the guy who pumps my gas. And SMILE . . . there . . . you look so much better!

When it comes to business formal, or personal introductions, things become a tad clearer. And while you may think it's difficult, it won't be if we all just use a little common sense.

There's really only one thing you need to remember. In the words of that great poet William Shakespeare: Rank hath its privileges. So if your boss walks in while you are speaking to the newbie in the department, you would stop the conversation and say Hi, Mr. Boss, I would like you to meet Newbie. Not the other way around, because Mr. Boss is more important. Likewise, let's say you are meeting a client for lunch and you are with one of your associates. Better yet, make it your boss. The client walks in, and of course you say Hello, Ms. Client, I would like to introduce you to Mr. Boss of my company. Since she is the one you are trying to woo or impress, she becomes the more important person as far as rank goes. Is this going to make or break your career? No. Is knowing to respect someone's position vis-a-vis others an enhancement and a differentiator? Absolutely!

And then there's always the introduction of your boyfriend when you run into Mr. and Mrs. Old Codger, lifelong family friends. Big smile in place, you greet them both and say, Mrs. OC, please meet David. Mr. OC, please let me introduce David. You would then go on to say that you know David from college. Depending on your relationship to the Codgers, you could embellish his curriculum vitae and then say he is

A) A very dear friend of mine.
B) My fiancée.
C) None of your business. (You wouldn't say it; you'd just say nothing.)

Remember that if it's "C" to just finish the pleasantries with, "It's nice to have seen you both," and be on your way.

Again, not that difficult. Just try to figure out or remember who the older, more important, or higher ranking individual is, and you'll see how easy introductions actually are.

But of course there are also the more simple introductions. Such as when you are at a cocktail party or when run into someone you haven't seen for a while or when you are just plain somewhere in which an introduction is in order. Then, it is more important just to make sure your friend, mother, or whoever gets introduced.

So many times people will say to me, "But what should I do if I forget their name?" Well, the worst thing, to me, is to not call someone by their name. And hey, even though I'm pretty good with names, because I have to be in my line of work, I still have my moments. The best example was when I was out to dinner with a friend at a local restaurant. He and I were having a lively conversation over drinks, and suddenly, this person comes over to me and says, "I would know that voice anywhere!" Now, I turn around and there stands a woman who looks familiar, and yet different. I reach back into the recesses of my mind and all of the friends, clients, colleagues, or what have you, and what comes to mind is, "Huh? Duh? Who the heck is this?"

The good news is that she knew my friend, whose son was her son's teammate back on the local high school football team. I go on and say to her, "This is my friend Jack," hoping against hope that she will (as a businessperson) say, "Oh, hey Jack, I'm Jill!" But no, that wasn't the case. Instead, they went on and on about her son, Tom Moore (oh yeah, Moore . . . big clue, Sue . . . hmmm . . . let me think of any Moore I might know) and his son, who's at Notre Dame, starting sophomore . . . hopefully on to the NFL . . . blah, blah, blah . . ., when suddenly it hits me, and I remembered her—Nancy Moore—my client who I haven't seen in five years. Yikes! Besides the fact that age has not been kind, I didn't even recognize her. So I partially recovered the potential fumble and said, Oh, Nancy, how's things at Big Fortune Company? Oh, yeah, sure, life is crazy busy for me too". And that was that. The moral of the story is that if someone introduces you and doesn't clearly state your name, please, please, do it yourself. Nancy could have stated her name and all would have been good.

Now, scenario number two is when Nancy is not a client. Just someone I may have known through life in general. The same thing happens, except I say to Nancy, "Please forgive me. I am so sorry, I know we've met but I'm just drawing a blank when it comes to your name." Perfectly fine in this case, since she is not a client or someone more important than me. But the nice thing to do is to still acknowledge my forgetfulness, and then be able to move on with the conversation.

Speaking of winning friends and influencing people, let's remember the guy who wrote the book on this stuff, Dale Carnegie. He's long gone, but his training franchises are still well and alive. Good old Dale was a proponent of self-improvement, good salesmanship, and interpersonal skills. One of the most important tenets of his teachings was about introductions and meeting people. The most basic rule is that when you meet someone, you should look them in the eye, give them a firm handshake, and then, while looking in their eye, repeat their name so you won't forget it. Let me tell you, this works more often than it fails. Obviously, relative to my story about Nancy, it occasionally does fail even the best of us. But sometimes life does get in the way. It's just good if we can minimize the times that it does.

If your eyes haven't glazed over by now, let's get on to the right handshake. The way you shake someone's hand says a lot about who you are. A handshake should be firm, not bone crushing. If I have numbness after a handshake, it's not good. It should be confident, not fishlike. If you hand me a three-finger handshake, I will presume you are sexist, and if you are a man, wimpy, and wimpy and uneducated if you are a woman. Do I sound a bit harsh? Good. Shaking hands is gender neutral. Period. End of story. I never said the presentation would be kid gloved. Oh, and while we are on the subject of gloves, if you are wearing them when you meet me, dude, please remove the right one when we shake hands. Yes. You would do Emily and Dale proud.

Chapter Twelve

Basic Table Manners: Aka How to Use a Napkin and Utensils, and Chew with Your Mouth Closed

M ost of you already know this stuff. I hope. But then again, I have to be honest—there are a lot of you that I watch when you are sitting next to me in a restaurant, using your forks and knives and spoons as if they were weapons.

Now, let's be honest. I'm not here to take you back to finishing school. I'm here to help you get ahead in the world by differentiating yourself from the herd. That's probably a good way of referring to some of the people I see. They eat like cattle. Yeah. Remember the cud-chewing cow we read about in Chapter Ten? The only difference is the intelligent look on the face of the cow.

So, if you haven't already, someday soon you will be asked to have lunch or dinner with your prospective boss. Yup. A lot of companies, especially those vetting peeps like you for the better jobs on The Street and in the Fortune 1000, will make breaking bread (aka dining together) a requisite of the talent challenge. And trust me. It's just not that hard.

Let's start with your napkin. A friend of mine is constantly telling her eighteen-year-old twin boys to put their napkins on their laps when they go out to eat together. "No, Mom," they reply in unison. "We'll do it when the food comes." At the risk of sounding like Emily Post, let me be clear: they are wrong! Once you sit down, you put it on your lap. Period. End of story. Duh. You might take a sip of water or inadvertently start buttering a piece of bread. That said, once you sit at the table, the napkin should be on your lap. (And please, do not mistake my tone for barking.) And that's where it stays, unless you are wiping your mouth. Or have to excuse yourself from the table. Which you will do using that exact word, as in "Excuse me, I will be right back"—not just I'm going to use the men's room, the ladies' room, call my girlfriend, mother, father, or whatever. Just "Excuse me, I will be right back." But before you leave, just remember to place your napkin gingerly (not throw it) on your chair (as in not on or near your plate). In a better restaurant, the waiter will take it, refold it, and then place it back at your place setting. Everywhere else, it's your responsibility to discreetly place it on your chair. And one more thing about napkins, in case you forgot: Don't ever let me see you blowing your nose in one. (You can do that in the restroom—add to the excuses for leaving the table.)

So, now that we have the napkin out of the way, let's move on to utensils. Need-to-knows that we will cover:

- The fork,the knife, the spoon
- The bread program: plate/butter knife/basket/how to eat
- The water glass
- The wineglass

Nice-to-knows that I won't bore you with:

- The fish fork
- The oyster fork

Well, we certainly do have our work cut out for us, don't we? Let's make it easy and fun.

Very simply, when it comes to utensils, work from the outside in. On the left side of your plate are your forks. The salad fork is to the left of the dinner fork. On the right side of the plate is your knife. And to the right of that would be a teaspoon or soupspoon. Easy-peasy. Forks on the left. Knife and spoons on the right. Work your way from the outside to the inside. Sometimes, though, the teaspoon and cake fork are positioned horizontally above the dinner plate, as in the image on the previous page. Obviously, since they are to be used for dessert, you would use those two pieces of silverware last.

Now that we've covered the logistics of the utensils, let's cover how to use them. As long as you are not holding your utensils like a caveman, you should be fine. In plain English, using your fist to hold a knife, fork, or spoon is base. And please, no draping them off the plate.

This is right:

This is wrong:

Where was you brung up, anyway? I hate teaching like we are at finishing school, but what the heck? I want you guys/girls to get the girl/guy/job/whatever because you stand out! A good friend of mine, very successful both personally and professionally, once said to me: "Good manners never go out of style." How right he is!

Is there really anybody out there who doesn't like, I mean love, bread? Especially the good crusty Italian bread they serve in all the restaurants that I go to? I know, I know, we shouldn't eat bread, or butter, for that matter, but the truth is we all do. So for goodness sake, get with the bread program.

The basics of the bread program are that your bread plate is on your left. Wherever you go, where there are civilized people, it will forever be on your left. Period. End of story. And don't give me that. How am I supposed to know? Like the guy I sat next to at the golf outing. And while I'm at it: bread on the left, drink on the right.

In better restaurants, or at my dinner parties, you will find a butter knife at the top of the plate, as if it were the top of the letter T. Since butter knives were invented to butter bread (that's all, just the bread, please) they are not sharp. They are only there to butter your bread. Please don't try to cut anything with them. Especially since we never cut bread, anyway. We break it into pieces, and then we butter it, as we eat it, only one piece at a time.

But, alas . . . I seem to have gotten a little ahead of myself.

Before we can even attempt to tackle the bread situation, we have to know how to pass the bread basket. By now, I know that you think I am a raving lunatic, but I don't care. I'm going to make all of you think about someone other than yourselves (as in the people around you). Because, dude, seriously, it's not all about you! Remember the title of this book? Well, it comes into play with the bread basket, too.

Let's play another one of my stupid (but educational) games.

The bread basket is in front of you. You:

A) Take a piece and pass it.
B) Pass it to your right so the person on your right goes first.
C) Pass it to your left so the person on your left goes first.
D) Who cares?

If you answered D, you can stop reading this book right now. Thanks for buying it, but you just don't care about anyone but you, so move on. For the rest of you, there is only one answer, which is C. You always pass to the left. And tough nuggies, you do not get to take a piece before you pass it. If the basket is in front of you, you have to pass it. Same goes for salt and paper (always passed together), lemons, etc. That's called good manners. I bet no one ever told you that before.

Now, when the basket comes around to you (if there is any bread left), just make sure you don't touch every last piece. Like Mom used to say: "You touch it, it's yours." And quite frankly, my dear, I don't give a damn if you don't like gorgonzola olive bread. You touched it, you own it.

So thank goodness, we can move on to water glasses and wineglasses. They are both on the right, and since your eyes are now glazing over with boredom (even though you are all going to make me so proud next time we go to dinner), suffice it to say, and in the interest of getting on with it, the wineglass is smaller than the water glass. And more importantly, the water glass is to the right of the wineglass. What else do you need to know? How much to drink? Don't even go there on an interview—no matter how much the prospective boss eggs you on.

If you are out with friends, in-laws, or family and not driving, a maximum of three drinks is reasonable. Out with friends and driving—no drinks. Period. End of story. I can't stop what you peeps will do at a frat party, but in the real world, the three-drink maximum is the rule.

And now on to nice-to-knows, that is, oyster forks, fish forks, and other sophisticated accessories. What I have found is that the more sophisticated an accessory, the more likely it is obvious what its intention is.

For example, back (way back) in the day, my grandmother would set her table with little crystal bars to the right of your plate. It was none other than a knife holder (LOL). She also had salt and pepper bowls, no more than a half inch wide, which were accompanied by little tiny minidollhouse-replica-sized silver spoons. It's pretty obvious that they were for the salt and pepper. And so it goes with oyster forks, which nowadays come along with your order of oysters. We rarely see fish forks anymore, other than in four-star restaurants, so the easiest way to understand where they are in the lineup is to pay attention to what is being served and in what order, and work from the outside in, as we talked about before.

The other thing you can do is take the lead of your host or hostess, which you are supposed to be doing anyway. We never start before they do. Them's the rules, 'cause, dude, seriously, it's not all about you. Not even at the table.

Bon Appétit!

Chapter Thirteen

Texting, Sexting, Drunk Texting, and Double Texting

Up until the new millennium, nobody had ever heard of texting. But since then, this new technology has become the go-to communication for many of us on the run. Texting is basically the exchange of brief written messages between landline phone or mobile phone and fixed or portable devices over a network. The problem is, as always, we sometimes forget who our audience actually is, and we abuse this method of communication, in more ways than one.

Just a few brief facts about texting (which will be outdated by the time you read this book) that, right now, we are sending about nine billion of them worldwide. And many of them are just a plain waste of your time and my time and your friends' time. I know, I know, you're a busy guy (or gal), but more importantly, you're important! If you need to get in touch with someone, you'd rather text than make a phone call (too time consuming, plus you would have to come up with a few pleasantries before you could actually start a conversation). On the other hand, why type an e-mail from your PDA when you can just look up your contact and send a quick text? Because, actually, some people still don't sign up for texting on their phone service. "Why," you ask? Because maybe they just don't want to be bothered with

anyone and everyone who happens to get hold of their mobile number. But enough pontificating on the merits (or not) of texting. Go ahead. Make your day. And text to a fare-thee-well.

Now, on to the people you are allowed to text:

- Your mother
- Your father
- Your sister
- Your brother
- Your cousins, aunts, and uncles (if they are not too old and know how to text you back)
- All of your BFFs
- Your boyfriend or girlfriend
- Your significant other
- Your husband
- Your wife
- Your business partner
- Your trainer

People, you should never text:

- Any of your clients
- Your boss

The only exception to the above is when you are specifically told that texting is an acceptable form of communication in your company.

Now that we have covered who we may appropriately text, let's move on to when we may not text. The first three are particularly important, as you can physically harm yourself or those around you. No texting:

- While driving—don't even think about it!
- While operating heavy machinery of any kind.
- While riding an escalator.
- At the breakfast table.

- At the lunch table.
- At the dinner table.
- In a meeting with a client.
- In a meeting with your coworkers.
- Any time or anywhere your attention should be on the human being you are with.

Now obviously, the world has changed. I know, I know, you simply are that important that you must be available to everyone, everywhere, 24/7. Right? Of course not. The truth is that texting is a valuable tool for all of us. Sometimes, for example, a quick text can let our date know we will be late or to change the location of a meeting point. But don't forget, our cell phones still allow us to communicate by talking, and sometimes that's just more appropriate (for example, if you are running late or changing a meeting location with a client). We just don't need to be sending three billion texts a day (collectively). Remember Rob (from Chapter Six), the guy who lives and breathes with the Bluetooth in his ear? Well, same concept here. It's annoying when I'm with someone, and they're vigorously typing away on their Blackberry while I'm trying to have a conversation with them. So unless you are in a college cafeteria or by yourself at the table, texting is unacceptable. That's all. If you follow that simple premise, you simply will not offend those around you. Remember the discussion we had about using your cell phone in a virtual office space? Well, texting in public is the same concept, with just a slightly different mode of communication. So, dude, seriously, think before you text. Sometimes a phone call (in a private space) works even better. Just follow the above sensibilities as to when, where, and with whom.

Remember, when you text while in the company of others, you're really saying to those accompanying you, "Hey, you're just not very important. It's all about me and whomever I'm texting, of course!" Is that really how you want to treat someone (even if you don't realize you're doing it)?

And, don't let me catch you sexting. Aw, c'mon, you all know what that is. So do Favre, Woods, and Weiner. And the rest of the world who read about them when they made headlines sexting the pretties they were hooking up with. To be clear, sexting is the act of sending sexually explicit messages or photographs, primarily between mobile phones. The term was first popularized around 2005 (*Wikipedia*).

Sexters generally resemble losers. The only peeps who might be allowed to sext each other would fall under the category of married. But still, we all know nothing necessarily lasts forever, so if you ask me, I still wouldn't let Mr. or Mrs. Right Now sext me verbally or via photograph, because breakups and divorces do happen. And they can be ugly. More importantly, it is likely that if things get nasty, anything they have in their possession can and very well may be used against you. Depending on your social status, those sexts could get into the wrong hands (aka lawyers' hands), and, well, you get it. And if you don't, well, don't come crying to me. Why? Because I told you so.

In the same category at sexting is drunk texting. *Urban Dictionary* defines drunk texting as follows: A modern derivative of its cousin, drunk dialing, this involves sending text messages via cell phone to friends, girlfriends, just friends, etc., while in a drunken stupor.

Typically, it is used on a desired member of the opposite sex, who is normally not desired during sober hours. This lame attempt to arrange a booty call results from the cowardice of the drunk texter, who fears actually making the drunk dial. Obvious clues that someone is drunk texting are really bad spelling, such as using a ton of LOLs, BAHAHAs, and other acronyms instead of real words.

Like sexting, the real problem with drunk texting is that if you make a horse's behind of yourself, that text can linger around on the other person's phone forever. You can cost yourself friendships, romances, and lots of embarrassment. So unless you think like Rhett Butler (aka Clark Gable's character in *Gone With The Wind*) and frankly just don't give a damn, put the phone away while you are imbibing and avoid acting like a complete fool.

Not nearly as bad from a legal standpoint, but certainly as annoying, is the concept of double texting. You know what it is. We've all done it. It's just that we all know someone who does it all the time!

They are just so dang involved in texting all of their friends, foes, parents, etc., that they are always sending the wrong text to the wrong person. Seriously, dude, if you are one of them, get a grip on yourself. Cut it out.

If you are still with me, I'm only going to say this once. Again. (LOL, you will pardon the expression.) No texting (ever) while driving or operating machinery. Need I say more? Get it? Got it? Good.

Chapter Fourteen

The Real World

Someday, when you go out into the real world, some of this stuff will start to be a lot more important than it seems right now. *Urban Dictionary* defines the real world as "What we live in. Touch your desk, punch your keyboard, stare at your monitor, work in your cubicle, drive home in bumper to bumper traffic, eke out a living, try to go out on the weekend with your friends, this is all part of the real world." As opposed to television, where there are things like a television show where seven strangers are placed in a mansion, with jobs, and free food and alcohol, and are constantly filmed for no other reason other than they are pretty, which is not the real world.

And then there's the world of teenagerdumb, which I am proud to say is my personal contribution to *Urban Dictionary*: The time of your life (varies, but usually the years between thirteen and nineteen . . . can last a lifetime for certain individuals) when you know everything better than everyone and you are invincible, infallible, and immortal. Also not part of the real world, but certainly a place where we've all been.

I should know, because I myself did some pretty dumb things when I was a teenager. Like the time I was in my senior year of high school, sitting in English class. It was a beautiful spring day, and nobody wanted to be inside. We started getting really rowdy and raucous, and suddenly, the teacher brought our antics to a screeching halt by saying, "Next person who says one more word is out, and goes down to the principal's office."

As if on cue, the words just flew out of my mouth, and I said: "ONE MORE WORD."

The class broke back into hysterics and the teacher merely said, "Susan, remove yourself from this classroom immediately and go see the principal."

How dumb could I be?

So the whole gist of the real world is that it's a place where the peeps you decide to engage with become your network. It's also the place where you get your first job, apartment, house, and ultimately, for most, partner (as in married or live-in partner). When you step out into the real world, which on some level starts in school, what you say and do, and how you treat those around you becomes the foundation for your life.

So hey, if you have grown up in a family where people scream and yell like banshees to get what they want, and it's worked for them, then I say go ahead and have fun seeing if that works in the real world. If it doesn't, it probably will be a painful process to change, but nothing that a great psychologist can't help with. And no, I am not being funny. I'm being serious. I've seen lots of people lose their jobs, their friends, and their marriages in the wake of bad behavior in the real world because they can't figure out that to be successful in the real world, treating people nicely is still a good thing. And as I like to say, the best revenge!

I am actually always taken aback when I see someone treating a salesperson, coworker, or friend/lover/spouse poorly in public. I can only imagine what the wrath they incur behind closed doors looks like, which reminds me of my own personal story.

Way back when, when I was the only girl/woman in the office (I say this because standing up to any of my coworkers during those days made me a b_tch), I had a coworker who was extremely jealous of me. He had been only an average (giving slightly more credit than is due) producer, and after my first year, I left him in the dust. Every time I would bring in a new client, he would try to steal them from me by making some flaky excuse, such as how he had known the person (blah, blah, blah), or he had tried to call the person (blah, blah, blah), or he was given that account last year and (blah, blah, blah). Well, you get the picture.

The real problem was that he was basically lazy or unmotivated—doesn't matter—and was always trying to get something to his credit without doing any of the work. So one day he pulls the stunt again. I go in to see my boss, and what does he say? My boss tells me that I have to understand how fragile the male ego is, and I just have to let it go. (Let it go? I incredulously say to myself, I think not!) Better yet, I'm gonna pull a sucker punch on him for all the times he's gotten away with trying to take what I had always worked so hard to produce. But I'm going to be so quiet, so subtle, and will so wait for the right time that he won't even know what hit him.

Only a few days had to go by when I met him in the coffee room. He started in on me about a new account I had just cracked. I was all ears listening to him berate me and tell me how I was infringing on his territory (which couldn't have been further from the truth because there actually were no territories in that office— only people who thought they were entitled to the fruits of someone else's labors). The louder he got, the more I listened, until I saw his face turning bright red and the veins popping out of his neck (like they did when he would have a fight with his wife, Jennifer, over the phone in front of all of us). When he finally stopped screaming, I simply looked at him and said, "Please don't talk to me the way you talk to Jennifer." That was it. It shocked him. He didn't know what to say. I filled my coffee mug, turned away, and walked back to my desk without another word and started my day, as usual, with my first marketing call. All the guys in the bull pen, and even my boss, didn't say a word. They knew that I had made my point, and if they ever wanted something from me in the future, they would have to speak to me like a mature adult.

That's just one example of the kind of stuff we have to handle in the real world. And we can be nice. We can be convicted. Or we can be babies and think that we're going to get our way by yelling, like my coworker did. I much prefer doing the right thing, even if I'm dealing with someone as lame as that guy. Simply put, I would not stoop to his level. I didn't scream back or rail at him. Why would I lower myself to his level? I have to admit that I was a bit patronizing, but at the same time, I simply wasn't going to take his nastiness. He never confronted me again and stayed out of my way from then on.

On the other hand, if you had a parent, relative, or mentor who knew how to charm and disarm those who crossed their path, and you've learned to emulate them, then you're way ahead of the pack.

I took the time to define the real world because that is where both good things and bad things happen. And we have to deal with all of them in the real world. So there are times when you are going to have to suck it up, and then there are times when you are going to have to stand up for yourself. The idea being that you always do so with grace and aplomb. That means be cool—no matter what.

Chapter Fifteen

Boundaries

What ever happened to them? That's my question. It seems like we don't have many, if any, anymore. Technology or people, it doesn't matter which. There are just no more boundaries!

The phone rings, and you've got to answer it. Your boss calls, you've got to jump. Text message comes through, answer it! E-mails popping up every second, you'd better hit the Reply button fast because you might miss something. Those are some examples of technology boundaries that we no longer have, because someone (I'm not sure who) somewhere decided that we have to be tethered to our PDA, cell, computer, or iPad. Maybe sometimes I just want to be incommunicado. Maybe sometimes I have to reflect a moment before I answer. And maybe sometimes I'm just plain busy.

Oddly enough, I'm starting to see a bit of backlash with boundaries in the technology spectrum. Part of it is that we get inundated all day long. And I know it's hard to believe, but busy, successful people just may be in meetings, lunches, taking power naps, or preparing a report for a client or superior—and actually, they may just be indisposed. So suck it up, and realize that people have priorities, and your need to know the answer to your question or the reply to your comment instantaneously may not be one of them. Note to self: it's not all about you!

But the boundaries that I really feel need review are the personal boundaries. You know the whole concept of familiarity breeds contempt? How about space invasion? How about having a little respect for people's privacy? Not everything is a need-to-know emergency. And by the way, when I'm in front of you, encroaching on me so I can feel (or worse, smell) your breath on my neck is just plain unacceptable. Oh, and one more thing. Let me finish my thought when I am talking, please. That's a boundary issue too. I finish. Then you go. This is the exchange method of communication (see Chapter Six).

So let's talk about boundaries in the workplace. You've just landed that new job. That new boss is so cool and hip. And the job—you will be working with some of the best and the brightest. The only thing you didn't factor in was the fraternization. The reason I know this is because I was a victim of it. Yup. It started very sneakily.

At first it was subtle, like the guys I worked with asking me to lunch. Of course, I had to go. I wanted to be accepted and part of the team. After that, it was, "Oh Joey's having some people over Friday night, you coming?" So of course, I said I would be there. They were fun guys (or so I thought), and so I dragged my husband along, who had absolutely nothing in common with these guys. So while he listened to their off-color jokes, I was relegated to hanging out with their wives, who worked inside the home. Not that there was anything wrong with that. It's just that I wasn't a mother yet, and listening to diaper talk was not my idea of an entertaining weekend night out. As far as I was concerned, watching paint dry would have been more fun. So, eyes glazed over, these fraternity parties became an expectation. Luckily for me, it didn't take long to figure out that I needed to put my own social calendar first. I showed up occasionally, so that I wouldn't become an outcast, but the Monday morning debriefings about what happened at the weekend party always confirmed what I very quickly learned from this experience, which is that familiarity breeds contempt. People were always gossiping. Jealousies abounded. I started thinking that I didn't belong there, and realized that someday when I had my own company, I would set boundaries for myself and my employees, which I did.

I loved (most of) the people that worked for me over the years. Yeah, we would have our celebratory dinners and parties, and every January we went off to some warm sunny clime for our company retreat. But somehow I never knew a lot of the little details that involved their children, spouses, or friends, unless they specifically came to discuss those things with me because they wanted my advice. I also didn't share with them some of my very personal trials and tribulations. No one was more surprised than they were when I tearfully announced my eminent separation and divorce from my husband of twenty-five years. Sure, they rallied around me, and I so appreciated that. But the down-and-dirty details—those I kept to myself. After all, I had a business to run and boundaries to protect.

So, if there's one thing you need to know when it comes to bosses and subordinates, it is this: familiarity breeds contempt. Whether you're the boss (and you have more love, money, or good times) or you're the subordinate (and you have more love, money, or good times), you open yourself up to other people's jealousies and insecurities, which in turn can affect your job, career, and/or livelihood. If you don't believe me, just watch a few episodes of *The Office* and you will see what I mean.

And now for one of my favorite subjects regarding boundaries: space invasion (done by an invader). The first kind of space invasion involves total strangers. Let me give you an example. I'm in the security line at Liberty International, aka Newark Airport, on Christmas Day. And don't let anybody fool you, Christmas Day has become one of the busiest travel days of the year. And we all know about the long lines and short tempers. So, anyway, back to my story. I leave what I consider to be a polite two feet between myself and the person in front of me. And then it starts. The (probably no more than) twelve-year-old girl behind me bumps into me. No "I'm sorry." I let it go. Two minutes later, she does it again. I realize her father is nudging her, as they are obviously very impatient or very late. Neither of which is my problem because the lines are up the wazoo. I give her a look. Well, maybe a dirty look. (Hey, I never said I was perfect, I'm just civilized.) But I stay patient and try to ignore her. The third time she does it, I turn to her as I glance at her father, and say in my most politely patronizing way, "Oh, did you want to go ahead of me?" Of course, that was a rhetorical question, with the rhetorical answer being no, as there actually was nowhere to go. It was then that her dad realized what a loser he was, and they backed off. No "I'm sorry" (see Chapter One). No "Pardon me." No "I didn't mean it." So do me a favor please, back off and realize that pushing me or breathing down my neck are not going to make the line any shorter. It's only going to make you an invader. And that's not a good thing.

The other kind of invader can be found in your office or at a cocktail party. The former nonchalantly hangs her head over your cubicle whenever she needs a break and just starts yacking without any regard for your (personal, albeit tiny) work space. The best thing to do, obviously, is to let her know that you are busy (doesn't usually work with these types) or working against a deadline, and you will catch up with her at lunch. (You can also excuse yourself and say you have to return a phone call.)

If you don't want to be known as an invader, the best thing to do when you interrupt someone who is obviously busy is to simply say, "Is this a good time?"

The second type of invader is the person you start talking to at a party (or anywhere, for that matter, but we will use the party example because I know how much fun all of you peeps are who are reading this book) who leaves no more than six to twelve inches between you and them. If they haven't brushed their teeth, you are definitely out of luck. If they have, you are still out of luck because they are just too dang close for comfort. What to do? My remedy is to keep backing up until I hit a wall or some other inanimate object, at which point I politely excuse myself for the bar.

The third type of invader is the guy who is all over your Facebook page making comments about you, messaging you, and just overall creeping you. The best thing to do is ignore this type. If it gets really bad, just put a message on your wall stating how much you hate FB creepers. Hopefully, he gets the message.

And now for the final boundary: stop interrupting when someone else is speaking. How many times have you started telling a friend or client (or whoever) a story, and, before you've finished two sentences, they are off and running. Talking over you. Not letting you finish. Not listening. Or worse yet, maybe it's the other way around. Maybe you're the one doing it. Either way, it's really annoying.

Personally, I work very hard to listen when someone is telling me something that I need to know, want to know, or am interested in. If, on occasion, I screw up and cut someone off, I apologize and say, "No, please, you go." On the other hand, if it's drivel, I usually just figure out a nice way to extricate myself from the conversation.

The best is when I initiate a call to a friend to share something that I am excited, sad, mad, or happy about. I start with, "Hey, it's me," and often they jump in without any regard for the fact that I placed the call. So here's my solution. In a very low voice I say, "Stop. Stop. Stop." That's how long it usually takes for them to stop. When they do, I simply say, "Hey, I called you, didn't I?" Once they stop and actually listen, I can tell my story. And when I'm done, it's their turn. The moral of the story is to listen, and don't talk over others when it's their turn. (See Chapter Six again. Listen. Exchange. Don't broadcast unless you're on the evening news!)

Chapter Sixteen

Body Modifications, Tattoos, and Your Skin: Aka Bod Mods, Tatts, and Your Skin

Just an FYI: I was one and a half when I had my ears pierced. That's what lots of Europeans did and still do (my parents were German). When I was in college, I came home with a second piercing on my left ear. Peace, love, and go-go boots! I was a rebel. I still have it, sometimes tout it—but quite frankly, I find it age inappropriate now. I cannot speak to tatts on a personal level, but a brother-in-law of mine who was in Vietnam back in the day, tattooed his arms and some of his chest, and came back to the real world and found he hated them. He had the procedure to de-ink himself, which resulted in lots of pain, lots of money spent, and lots of tatts still showing (just a little lighter in tone).

I know, I know, I'm a small-minded conservative who thinks they are disgusting. Not at all. Just make sure you under-stand that once they are inked, they will be there for posterity. So unless you are a rock star, tattooing a sleeve on both arms will probably be a bit of a gamble when it comes to knowing for sure that you want it on your body for the rest of your life. Piercings I'm not so down on because you can just remove the metal object and no one will be the wiser. Moral of the story:

we change, times change, but tatts don't go away. Which brings me to your skin. One thing I know for sure is that if you're going to own any tatts, make sure they are not showing in public at your nine-to-five job. Go ahead and make your statement if it makes you feel better. Just don't let anyone see them during office hours. It's not good for the fast track.

So, no tramp stamps, sleeves, or any obvious tatts. Ditto for cleavage, thongs, or butts. Additional moral of the story: think before you ink. Go ahead and put holes all over your body. Just don't stick any metal into them while at the office.

Oh, and one more thing. We are (well, most of us anyway) not porn stars, so if your Vickie's Secrets or Calvin Kleins are peeking out, do us all a favor and save them for your intimate moments. Note to self: Check definitions for Intimate Departments and Underwear Departments.

Chapter Seventeen

Profanity

I'm not going to lie. I am sick and tired of hearing people swear in public. Parents swear at or in front of their kids at the grocery store. People yell curse words at each other when they don't agree or are arguing about something. And the worst is that too many of you guys/girls who are reading this (you'll pardon the classifications youngsters and adolescents) think it's perfectly fine to sprinkle profanity in every sentence. Well guess what? It's not. It's gross. It cheapens who you are and will impact the success you can achieve. So go ahead, if you want to be a middle-aged dude who runs around saying "f__ this" and "f__ that," be my guest. If that's the only way you can get noticed, go for it.

If you learned to be profane from your parents because that's how they communicate, defy them. Yes, you heard me—just don't mirror their bad habits. And guess what, I guarantee you that they will never notice, as they are totally wrapped up in their own bad behavior. Not to dis your parents, but it's not going to differentiate you in the real world. Yeah, you remember the real world. The place where we all go after school, where getting a good job and a great spouse, and raising a decent family are the goals for most of us reading this book.

Point to be taken: what you think is cool today will not (always) be cool twenty or thirty years from now. It certainly won't be cool in your first job. Is this what we call respecting ourselves, families, friends, and people, in general? I think not. I won't spend two more seconds on this subject because I know I'm right. If you disagree, go for it. It's ultimately your life to lead as you wish!

Chapter Eighteen

Gentlemen...
Please Remove Your Hats

I know, I know. Who cares? Do you remember when a man tipped his hat when he saw a woman on the street or when a man walked into a restaurant or your house and automatically removed his hat? Back in the day? Okay, so maybe you don't and maybe no one in your immediate circle cares. Well, guess what? I do. Because, I want you to stand out from the herd when it comes to doing the right thing.

I don't know who made up the rule or why. I just know that there are still people out there who will judge you by the little things that make you stand out—good and bad— right and wrong. It's a fact.

Remember, this book is all about differentiating yourself. You can be an average schmoe or you can be a lady or a gentleman. The choice is yours.

My friend Lynn and I were debating this topic over cocktails, and she pointed out to me that people will do what they want. However, to those of us who have been taught how to behave in a certain way, we will know immediately how another person was raised by their actions. And, yes, we care because we want to hang out with like-minded folks. In this case, respectful types.

As my grandmother (the one who wanted me to be able to dine with the Queen of England) said, "Suzi, you can go anywhere when you have manners, even if you are not rich."

What she meant was that if you were rich but boorish, you would find certain doors closed to you. Personally, I would prefer to be respectful and mannerly AND rich.

Here's a scenario for you. Your boss's boss takes you to his swanky golf club and you walk into the clubhouse and don't remove your cap. The club manager walks over and discretely asks you to. (And, that rule is gender neutral, ladies, because caps are unisex.) Embarassing, right? Well, like I always say, it's truly the little things that count. Yours is not to question why. Yours is just to do or...maybe just not to get asked back as a member's guest.

Also, ladies and gentlemen, you don't wear a cap during the singing of the national anthem. It's disrespectful to Old Glory (the United States Flag).

On the other hand, it's quite alright to wear hats and caps in public places...such as elevators and hallways. It's PUBLIC, that's why...every man's/woman's space.

But, gentlemen, you never wear your cap/hat in restaurants, theaters, or the like. Why? Because people pay to go there and expect to see a modicum of decorum and respect. Ladies MAY where their hats in a restaurant or theater, but if your hat is blocking someone's view of the stage, then the right thing to do would be to remove it so that the peeps behind you can enjoy the show, too.

And, for the final word on hats and ladies. Ladies, you actually may wear a hat (but not a cap) in club houses, places of worship, and during the singing of the national anthem. Note the distinction. I repeat. Never a *cap*, but *hats* are okay.

You don't agree? No problem. Just don't be sitting next to me in a restaurant or I will ask the waiter to have you remove your cap!

Recap

Respect (from dictionary.com): to hold in esteem or honor (*I cannot respect a cheat*); to show regard or consideration for (*to respect someone's rights*); to refrain from intruding upon or interfering with (*to respect a person's privacy*); to relate or have reference to.

If you got this far, you were curious, skeptical, incredulous, or interested. All of which are possibilities. If you took one thing away, anywhere in this book, then my rant was worth it.

The truth of the matter is that whether you are an arrogant, pompous ass, a well-bred debutante, a student or a teacher, a child or a parent, a friend, or even an enemy, the world needs all of us to have or show a little more respect.

So whether you decide to hold the door for the person behind you or stop the road rage or mince your profanity or stop yawning in my face, these small acts of respect will go a long way to charming and disarming those around you. You will give a little and find that you will get a lot more in return. And mostly, you will find that being nice is still the best revenge, and that knowing how to treat people well (aka having good manners) never goes out of style.

Resources

Decision Points, by George W. Bush, Crown, Nov. 9, 2010.

http://dictionary.reference.com/, Dictionary.com, LLC,
    Oakland, CA.

Etiquette in Society, in Business, in Politics, and at Home, by Emily
    Post, Funk & Wagnalls Company, New York, 1922.

How to Win Friends and Influence People, by Dale Carnegie, Simon &
    Schuster; Reissue edition, Nov. 3, 2009.

http://www.urbandictionary.com/, Urban Dictionary, LLC,
    San Francisco, CA.

http://www.wikipedia.org/, Wikimedia Foundation Inc.,
    San Francisco, CA.

About the Author

© JanPress/PhotoMedia

Susan P. Ascher is an author, professional speaker, and award-winning business owner. A graduate of Lehigh University, Susan has spent 30 years in the staffing industry and is the creator of The Developmental Sphere of Excellence in Communications, her response to the outcry from her clients to help in differentiating their teams through better communications and respect for coworkers, superiors, and subordinates. In addition to her work in the corporate world, Susan coaches students at major universities and colleges on the necessary "real-life" protocol needed to find their path in a highly competitive job market and a 24/7 technology-driven world.

Susan's irreverent sense of humor and authentic style are both charming and disarming. A riveting orator, Susan speaks on a variety of topics that provide real-life examples about the challenges and successes that face us in our everyday existence as well as life in the workplace and the world at large. This book is not about your grandmother's or Miss Manner's rules regarding tennis whites and oyster forks . . . this book shares Susan's insights on how treating people well and with respect can make you a rock star in the real world, no matter who you are: parent, student, leader, friend, or spouse.

Susan has seen the workplace, schools, and main street evolve from a state of civility and human engagement to places where many hide behind technology and the excuse of "not having the time" to be respectful. She shows people how going back to the basics in human contact go a long way to enjoying better relationships, better jobs, and a better life.

A sought-after national media resource, Susan is a regular presenter at outplacement firms specializing in professionals in transition. She is a frequent commentator on TV 8 in Vail, Colorado and been interviewed on *Bloomberg, ABC, NBC, CNBC, News 12*, and *My9TV*. Susan has presented workshops at universities throughout the country, such as Colorado Mountain College in Edwards, Colorado; William Paterson University in Wayne, New Jersey; and Fairleigh Dickinson University, in Florham Park, New Jersey.

She has been interviewed and published in *Forbes* magazine, *Crain's New York Business, The Star-Ledger, NJBIZ*, and *New Jersey & Company* magazine.